This journal
belongs to:

HOW WAS YOUR DAY?

A Journal for Everyday Wonders

By Bridget Watson Payne

CHRONICLE BOOKS
SAN FRANCISCO

Bridget Watson Payne is an artist, writer, book editor, and the author of *How Art Can Make You Happy*. She is based in San Francisco. See more of her work at bridgetwatsonpayne.com.

ISBN 978-1-4521-6997-2

MIX
Paper from
responsible sources
FSC
www.fsc.org   FSC™ C137129

Manufactured in China
Illustrations by Bridget Watson Payne

10 9 8 7 6 5 4 3 2 1

Chronicle Books publishes distinctive books and gifts. From award-winning children's titles, bestselling cookbooks, and eclectic pop culture to acclaimed works of art and design, stationery, and journals, we craft publishing that's instantly recognizable for its spirit and creativity. Enjoy our publishing and become part of our community at www.chroniclebooks.com.

Special quantity discounts are available to corporations and other organizations. Contact our premiums department at corporatesales@chroniclebooks.com or at 1-800-759-0190.

Chronicle Books LLC
680 Second Street
San Francisco, California 94107
www.chroniclebooks.com

INTRODUCTION

The world is full of fleeting marvels. "Blink, and you'll miss it," people say, but really, you don't even have to blink. Life comes at you fast, and you've got to tune out a lot of stuff or you'll go bonkers from overstimulation.

What that can mean is that at the end of the day, when some nice friend or family member asks you over the dinner table, "How was your day?" your mind goes blank and you barely know the answer to the question. Sure, you can probably offer up that it was an unusually good day, or an unusually bad day, or an unusually boring day, if such was the case. But the details are already very nearly all gone.

The tiny magical gifts life offers us throughout our days escape us, and we're left with the broad outlines. We might have a story about some annoying thing that happened, but other than that, we're not much different from the five-year-old who's asked, "What did you do in school today?" and who inevitably answers, "Stuff."

Paying attention to the world around us and the world inside us is a way of taking care of ourselves. When we tune in to our senses—to all the myriad things we see and hear and taste and feel with our bodies in a day—we are grounding ourselves in our lived reality. When we pay attention to the inner workings of our minds—all the thoughts we think and emotions we feel through-out the day—we are honoring our unique and individual selves.

The day you will walk through today is one of a kind. To capture it, all you have to do is look.

Choose a page in this journal. You can pick one at random, search through for one that particularly speaks to you, or just work through the book from start to finish. Whichever you choose, take a moment to think back on your day and locate the answer to the question that page is asking you.

Then spend a few minutes journaling. First, describe the thing you saw or heard or felt in some detail. Then, write about why it stood out to you, what made it special, and maybe even what it meant in the larger context of your day.

Believe your life is worthy of being seen, and watch the magic happen.

LET'S GET
STARTED!
THE WORLD
AWAITS.

SOMETHING BEAUTIFUL I SAW TODAY

_____

DATE

WHAT I HAD FOR BREAKFAST TODAY

_____

_____

_____

_____

_____

_____

_____

_____

_____

_____

_____

_____

_____

_____

DATE

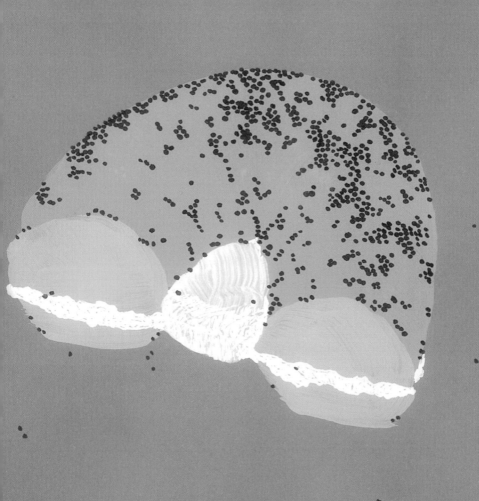

MUSIC I LISTENED TO TODAY

_____

_____

_____

_____

_____

_____

_____

_____

_____

_____

_____

_____

_____

_____

_____

_____

DATE

SOMETHING SOFT I TOUCHED TODAY

DATE

A CHILDHOOD MEMORY
I THOUGHT OF TODAY

_____

_____

_____

_____

_____

_____

_____

_____

_____

_____

_____

_____

DATE

AN ACT OF LOVE
I ENCOUNTERED TODAY

_____

_____

_____

_____

_____

_____

_____

_____

_____

_____

_____

DATE

SOMETHING DELICIOUS
I TASTED TODAY

_____

_____

_____

_____

_____

_____

_____

_____

_____

_____

_____

_____

_____

_____

DATE

A VEHICLE I SAW TODAY

_____

_____

_____

_____

_____

_____

_____

_____

_____

_____

_____

_____

_____

DATE

BEST THING I SMELLED TODAY

_____

_____

_____

_____

_____

_____

_____

_____

_____

_____

_____

_____

_____

DATE

THE SADDEST THING
I ENCOUNTERED TODAY

DATE

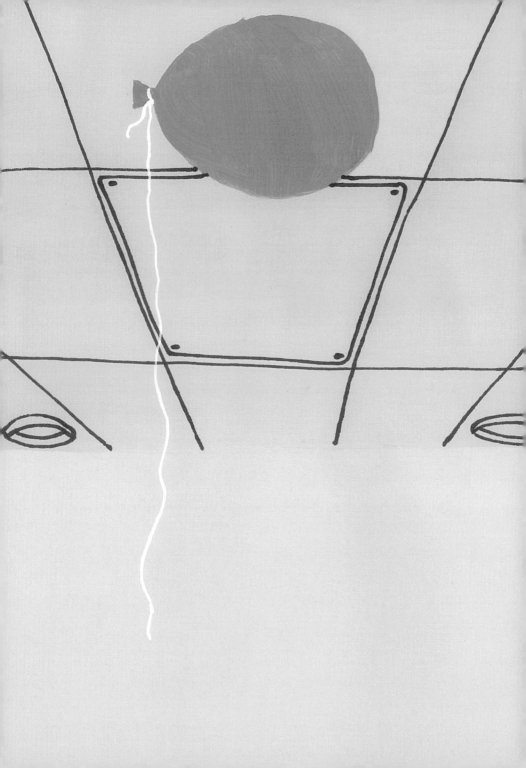

THE SOUNDS OUTSIDE
MY WINDOW TODAY

_____

_____

_____

_____

_____

_____

_____

_____

_____

_____

_____

_____

_____

_____

DATE

THE BIGGEST THING I SAW TODAY

_____

_____

_____

_____

_____

_____

_____

_____

_____

_____

_____

_____

_____

_____

_____

_____

_____

_____

_____

_____

_____

_____

DATE

THE MOST FUN I HAD TODAY

_____

_____

_____

_____

_____

_____

_____

_____

_____

_____

_____

_____

DATE

A FLAVOR I ENCOUNTERED TODAY

_____

_____

_____

_____

_____

_____

_____

_____

_____

_____

_____

_____

_____

DATE

FAVORITE ARTICLE OF CLOTHING
I WORE TODAY

_____

_____

_____

_____

_____

_____

_____

_____

_____

_____

_____

_____

DATE

SOMETHING THAT MADE ME
LAUGH TODAY

DATE

SOMETHING UNIQUE I HEARD TODAY

_____

DATE

THE HARDEST THING I DID TODAY

_____

_____

_____

_____

_____

_____

_____

_____

_____

_____

_____

_____

_____

DATE

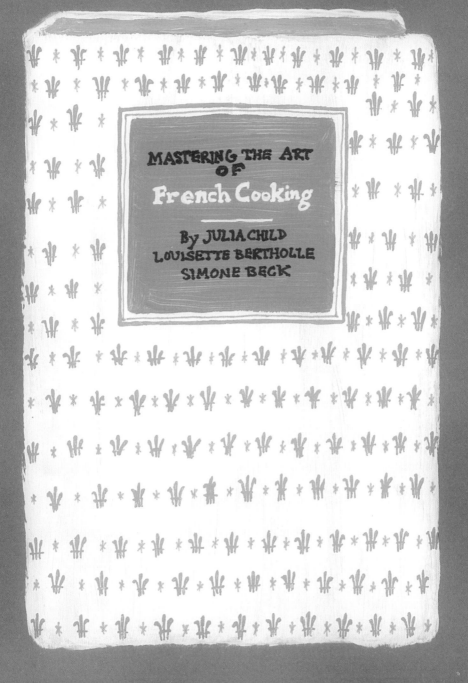

SOMETHING I SAW LOOKING UP TODAY

DATE

SOMETHING SALTY I ATE TODAY

_____

DATE

THE EASIEST THING I DID TODAY

_____

_____

_____

_____

_____

_____

_____

_____

_____

_____

_____

_____

_____

_____

_____

DATE

A GUILTY PLEASURE
I ENJOYED TODAY

DATE

AN EMOTION I FELT TODAY

DATE

SOMETHING TRUE I LEARNED TODAY

_____

_____

_____

_____

_____

_____

_____

_____

_____

_____

_____

_____

_____

_____

DATE

Bad Feminist | Essays | Roxane Gay

HARPER PERENNIAL

COMFORT ME WITH APPLES | RUTH REICHL

RANDOM HOUSE

JUST KIDS | PATTI SMITH

CCCO

OVERWHELMED | BRIGID SCHULTE

PICADOR

Men Explain Things to Me | REBECCA SOLNIT

JANET MOCK | REDEFINING REALNESS

ATRIA

THE MOST COMFORTING THING
I DID TODAY

_____

_____

_____

_____

_____

_____

_____

_____

_____

_____

_____

_____

_____

_____

_____

_____

DATE

AN INTERESTING BUILDING
I SAW TODAY

_____

_____

_____

_____

_____

_____

_____

_____

_____

_____

_____

_____

DATE

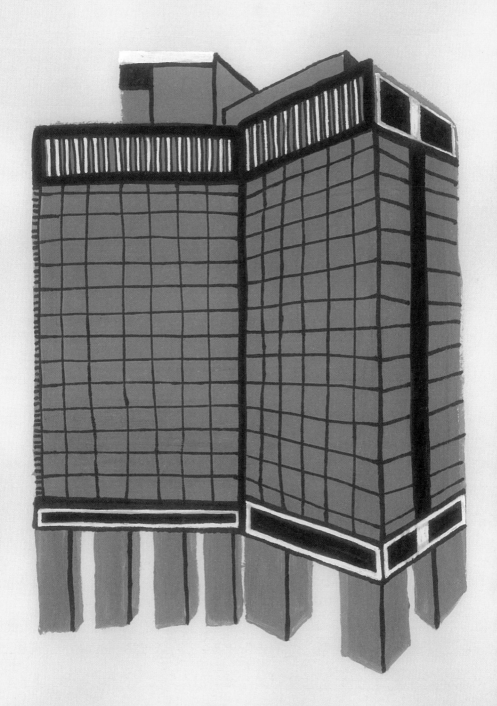

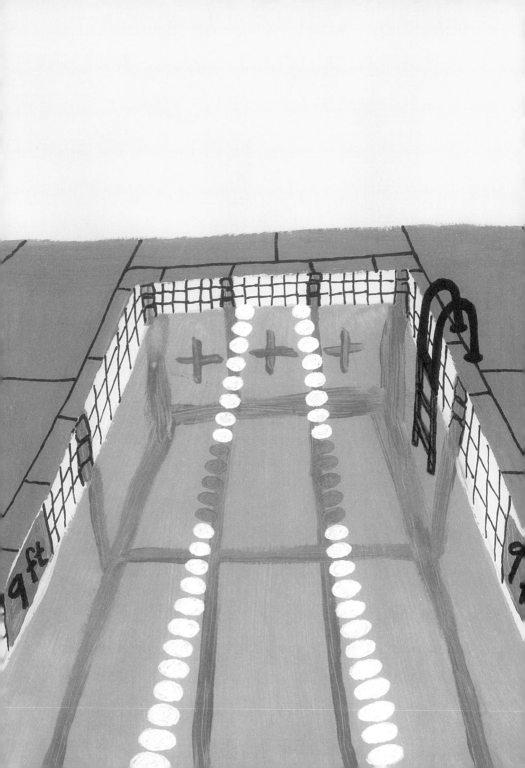

SOMETHING PHYSICAL I DID TODAY

DATE

A VOICE I HEARD TODAY

_____

_____

_____

_____

_____

_____

_____

_____

_____

_____

_____

_____

_____

_____

_____

_____

_____

DATE

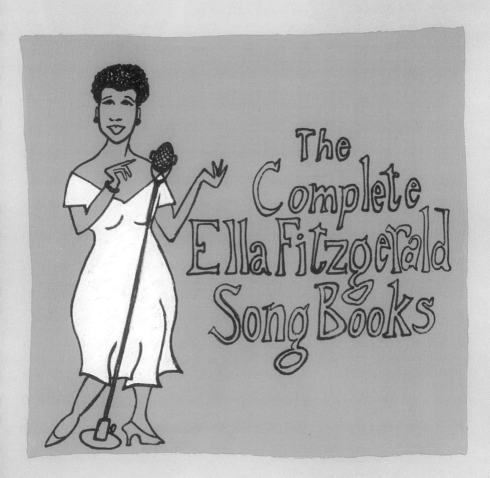

SOMETHING ANALOG I USED TODAY

DATE

A GLIMPSE OF NATURE I HAD TODAY

_____

_____

_____

_____

_____

_____

_____

_____

_____

_____

_____

_____

_____

_____

_____

_____

_____

_____

DATE

THE BEST IDEA I HAD TODAY

_____

_____

_____

_____

_____

_____

_____

_____

_____

_____

_____

_____

_____

_____

DATE

SOMETHING I WAS
GRATEFUL FOR TODAY

DATE

SOMETHING BLUE I SAW TODAY

_____

_____

_____

_____

_____

_____

_____

_____

_____

_____

_____

_____

_____

_____

DATE

THE FIRST THING I HEARD TODAY

_____

DATE

THE FASTEST THING I DID TODAY

_____

_____

_____

_____

_____

_____

_____

_____

_____

_____

_____

_____

_____

_____

_____

DATE

A TIME WHEN MY MIND
WAS CALM TODAY

_____

_____

_____

_____

_____

_____

_____

_____

_____

_____

_____

_____

DATE

SOMETHING I FORGOT TODAY

_____

_____

_____

_____

_____

_____

_____

_____

_____

_____

_____

_____

_____

DATE

THE BEST THING
I HAD TO DRINK TODAY

DATE

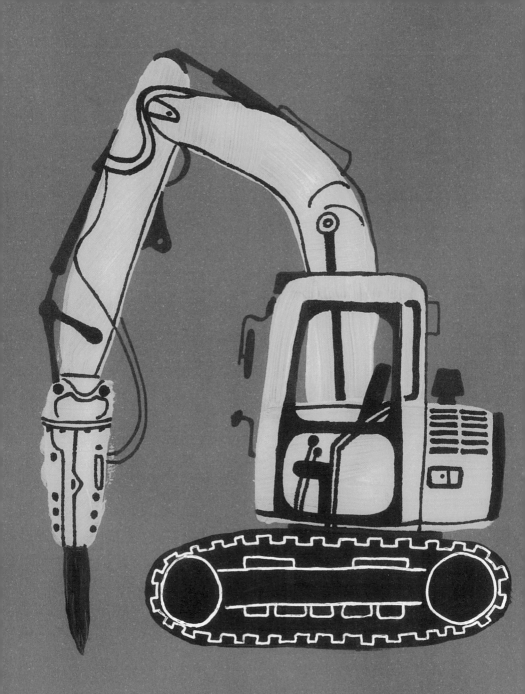

THE LOUDEST THING
I ENCOUNTERED TODAY

DATE

SOMETHING THAT CHALLENGED ME TODAY

DATE

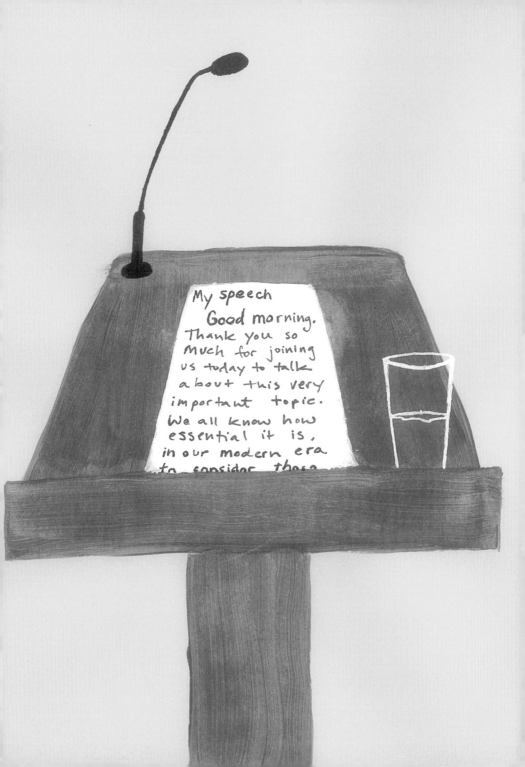

SOMETHING CUTE I SAW TODAY

DATE

A SCENT THAT REMINDED ME OF SOMETHING TODAY

DATE

THE LEAST-MEMORABLE THING
I ATE TODAY

_____

_____

_____

_____

_____

_____

_____

_____

_____

_____

_____

_____

_____

DATE

WHERE MY MIND WANDERED TODAY

DATE

SOMETHING COLORFUL I SAW TODAY

DATE

A MOMENT OF PEACE
I EXPERIENCED TODAY

_____

_____

_____

_____

_____

_____

_____

_____

_____

_____

_____

_____

_____

_____

_____

_____

_____

DATE

THE BEST SOUND I HEARD TODAY

_____

_____

_____

_____

_____

_____

_____

_____

_____

_____

_____

_____

_____

_____

DATE

THE SLOWEST THING I DID TODAY

_____

_____

_____

_____

_____

_____

_____

_____

_____

_____

_____

_____

DATE

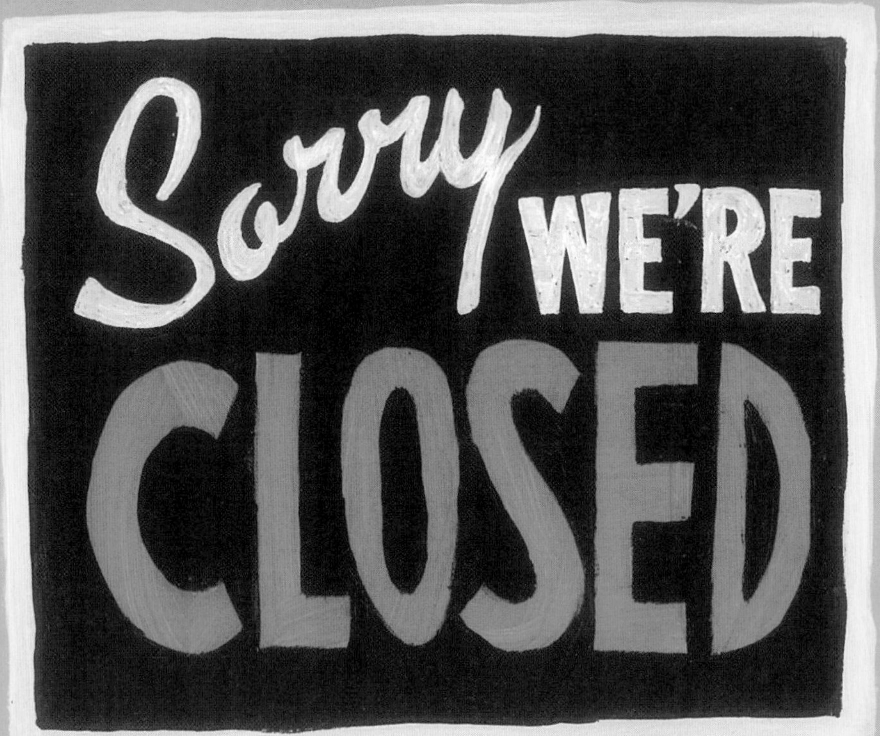
Sorry WE'RE
CLOSED

SOMETHING I REALIZED TODAY

_____

_____

_____

_____

_____

_____

_____

_____

_____

_____

_____

_____

_____

_____

_____

_____

_____

DATE

SOMETHING THAT MADE ME
HAPPY TODAY

_____

_____

_____

_____

_____

_____

_____

_____

_____

_____

_____

_____

DATE

Hope
today is
a good
one!